ENDORSEMENTS

"Thanks for playing really fun games to help me learn. It's cool that you have a Bible on your phone!"
(4TH GRADE BOY)

"I like knowing that what we tell you is completely confidential to our group. Thank you for not judging us based on what we tell you. I like it that I care about your opinion a lot. I really respect you on a very high level."
(10TH GRADE GIRL)

"I miss you. You were my small group leader in preschool. You have the best hugs and the best smile. That's why I still visit you."
(2ND GRADE BOY)

"You help me connect to God in a fun way on like a personal and enjoyable level. You like, relate to us and help us follow God's path . . . with swag."
(8TH GRADE BOY)

"I want to model myself after you. I look up to you. The morals that you hold us to are the same morals you hold personally. I love how we can confide in you and know that not only are we going to get solid advice, but you support us even through our mistakes."
(12TH GRADE GIRL)

"You influenced me because you invested in me relationally. You knew my interests. You knew my hobbies. You were right there and got to know my family. You were the guy who could say, "Yea, that's dumb," or "That's not good for you," and I would listen. You modeled what it was like to be a small group leader. That kind of made me become interested in ministry because I watched you do it."

(25 YEAR-OLD MAN, WHO NOW LEADS A 6TH GRADE SMALL GROUP)

COPYRIGHT

DEDICATION

This book is dedicated to all the small group leaders everywhere. For all the early Sunday mornings, all the late, late Friday nights, the sugar highs and the emotional lows, the sticky hugs and the difficult phone calls. Thank you for your commitment to the next generation.

ABOUT THIS BOOK

After almost 50 years of combined ministry experience, we knew we wanted to write a book to small group leaders. We saw two possible ways of achieving that goal. We could either go out and find the single most incredible small group leader on the planet and ask them to write a book, or we could create a team of small groups leaders and draw from their collective experiences. For their creativity, their transparency, and their commitment to live out this idea of leading small, we would like to thank Abbey Carr, Eryn Erickson, Kristen Ivy, Cara Martens, Kristie McCollister, Matt McKee, Sue Miller, Courtney Templeton, Lauren Terrell, Jeremy Zach and Mikaela Zach.

HOW TO USE THIS BOOK

As a guide for small group leaders of all ages, we realize not all the topics and examples will apply evenly across the board. As students grow, the role of a small group leader changes. Some practices that we ask of a preschool leader, we would never encourage from a student leader. And some things a good student leader will do, would be entirely inappropriate at the preschool stage. As you go through this book, you will notice journal sections intended to help you put some of your own ideas into practice.

Look for the P, C and S to help you figure out how each topic can apply specifically for the age group you lead.

Preschool   Children   Students

FOREWORD

So, you're in charge of a small group of kids.
(Well, not "in charge" . . . that's really their parents.)

So, you teach a small group of kids.
(Actually, their teachers and coaches really do that . . .)

So, you hang out with a small group of kids.
(No . . . their friends really have that covered.)

So, what *do* you do? Where do you fit? What is your role?

And even more, *why*?

Actually, those exact questions are probably why you bought this book. Or, more likely, were given this book by your church. Or, even *more* likely, picked it up thinking it was a guide for *leading* your *small* plastic green army men to victory over the dangerous barrel of monkeys.

In the latter case, this is not the book for you. Put the book down. Try the "Gaming" section. It's probably on the lower shelves.

For all others, this is your handbook, your user guide, your journal.
Read it.
Contemplate it.
Personalize it.

Let's get started.

TABLE OF CONTENTS

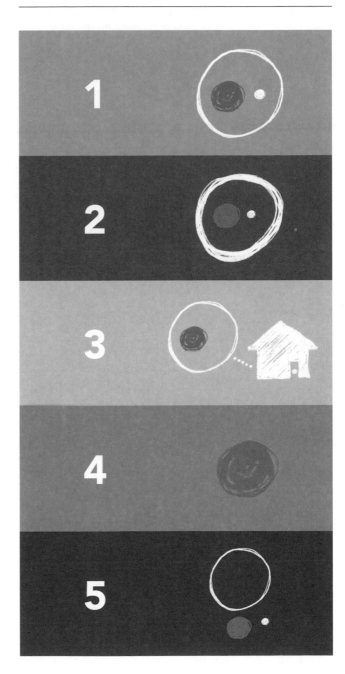

big
challenge

BIG CHALLENGE.
SMALL SOLUTION.

We have a challenge. A BIG challenge. Most studies today indicate that at least half of students will walk away from their faith in college. Why?

Pushy professors?
Radical roommates?
Cynical sweethearts?

Although these may be the easy mark, the real culprit starts long before English 101. It's not something they come across on campus. It's not lying in wait beneath dorm room lofts.

It's something they bring from home. It's packed in their bags next to their "shower shoes," beneath the keepsake from a nearly forgotten high-school romance.

It's a pseudo, immature, green, borrowed or fragile faith.

Now, before you start the blame game, we, as parents and leaders in their lives, didn't necessarily fail them. Think about their stage of life.

They are young.
They have a lot to learn.
A long way to go.
They have yet to experience life at its fullest.

Their faith is, to some degree, **unchallenged.**

So, now that you understand the BIG challenge, what's the solution?

This is where you come in. Your goal is to raise kids with a stronger faith—with what we call authentic faith.

If you're wondering what that looks like,
it's probably something like what Paul described when he wrote to Timothy:

"Okay son, listen up because you are out on your own now—ready to do what God called you to do. You will need to hold onto the commands I'm giving you so that you can fight a good fight. Hold onto faith. Have a good conscience. Don't reject them and suffer like others have done,"
(1 Timothy 1:18-19, RJLT).[1]

Isn't that what we are after? We want a generation to grow up holding onto a faith that is rooted in scripture. We want kids who place their trust in God, not only
In a moment
At VBS
On the last night of camp

But *every day.*

We want them to have a really **BIG** faith—an authentic faith.

And the only way you can cultivate authentic faith is through leading **SMALL**.

---

[1] RJLT = Reggie Joiner Loose Translation. This is not a real translation.

lead
small

Lead Small

"What do you mean 'lead *small*'?"
"Shouldn't I make a BIG difference?"
"What about changing the world?"

Most people dream of finding an opportunity to do something BIG.
To make a BIG change.
To lead BIG.

That's why we . . .
Accumulate Facebook friends and Twitter followers
Make videos in hopes of going viral
Climb the corporate ladders
Audition for "So You Think You Have the Voice to Dance with the Biggest Loser."

In fact, most of us believe—

The best way to make a
BIG difference is to get a
big following.

And when the masses don't follow,
when the 11 o'clock news isn't knocking down the door ...

We try something else.
Something BIG.
Like dancing on an over-sized keyboard with Tom Hanks.

But . . .

What if the things we consider BIG
Don't matter as much as we think?

What if the biggest difference is made
By not doing something big at all?

What if the biggest things are really accomplished
By doing something **SMALL**?

If we aren't careful,
we can work so hard at leading big
we never experience the power
of leading small.

When we lead small we realize
that what we **do for a few** will always have more potential
than what we do for many.

When we lead small we simply make a choice to invest strategically in the lives of a few over time so we can help them build an authentic faith.

We lead small to build authentic faith.

It's the principle this book is dedicated to.

You are the person this book is dedicated to.

You are a **SMALL** group leader.

You had the courage to think **SMALL** enough to take on the BIG challenge.

You chose to invest in the few lives in your group.

And while group members come in all sizes—
Those who wear pampers
Those who watch Disney
Those who have squeaky voices
Those who are learning to drive
Those who are picking a college—

Every size, every age, needs the kind of influence you have the potential to give.

But what exactly do you do?

What exactly is your role?

You may feel lost at times, like you fall somewhere between a parent and a friend, a coach and a teacher. Remember, you aren't supposed to be *any* of those things. You are a little of *all* of those things.

You're a little bit of a friend, parent, coach, *and* teacher combined. Let's say you're a Friend . . . Poacher?

No, that's bad. Let's just stick with small group leader. Or **SGL**.

And when we say SGL, we are talking about anyone who chooses to invest in the lives of a few to encourage authentic faith.

As you read this book, you will discover how to . . .

BE PRESENT
CREATE A SAFE PLACE
PARTNER WITH PARENTS
MAKE IT PERSONAL
MOVE THEM OUT

Even more, you will understand how these five strategies will encourage the personal, vibrant, passionate, tested, living, authentic faith needed to face our big challenge. And why the only way to fully invest in these strategies is by leading **SMALL**.

As you read, you will also notice a few important graphics.

 A circle represents a group. Not a group of wild boar. (Although, they may seem to be at times.) A group of students or kids. And not just any group. *Your* group.

 A large orange dot represents YOU. The SGL. Don't you look good?

 A small dot represents one individual in your circle. Someone you are leading.

 A home represents . . . well, a student's home. What else would it be?

A dotted line is just a dotted line. I think you get the point.

So, I guess we're done. Now you know absolutely all you need to know to be a good SGL. You have all the tools you'll need: a circle, two dots, a home, and a dotted line.

So, go out and lead
Invest.
Encourage.
Change lives.

No? Things still a little fuzzy? Okay, okay. I'll explain a little more.

1

be
present

**CONNECT THEIR FAITH
TO A COMMUNITY**

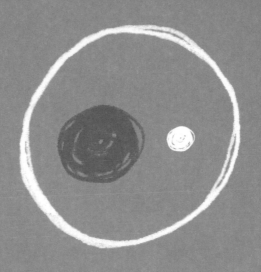

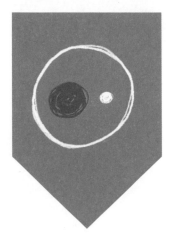

be
present

**CONNECT THEIR FAITH
TO A COMMUNITY**

When God made man, Adam was alone in Eden—what has since become the icon of perfection.

Peaceful.
Tranquil.
Eden.
—And Adam.

But it wasn't perfect, was it?
Adam was immersed in lush vegetation of all kinds.
He was surrounded by hundreds of different living species.
But Adam was still lonely.

The vines made lousy dance partners.
The hyenas were poor conversationalists. (They laughed at their own jokes! Who does that?)
The elephants were (not so surprisingly) dreadful at hide-and-seek.

But God understands the human need to connect.
God created us with a need for community.
God knew it wasn't good for man to be alone.
God made Eve.

Fast-forward thousands of years.
God came to Earth as man.
At the beginning of Jesus' ministry He chose twelve guys.
He didn't invite the masses.
His goal was not to fill the largest amphitheater in Corinth.
He led thousands but chose to invest in, to do life with, a few.

Understanding the human need for community, and its significance in our lives, Jesus surrounded Himself with a few deep relationships. In doing this, Jesus connected the faith of the twelve. And after Jesus was no longer on Earth to lead them, the disciples were able to stay strong in their faith because it was connected to others.

STILL NOT CONVINCED? LET'S GO A STEP FURTHER.

Fifty years passed and Paul was busy setting up the Church in cities across the known world—building the Church around this concept of community.

The earliest churches had no buildings.
No choir rooms.
No praise band.

There were no kids' programs.
No Sunday school classes.
No fall festivals.

There was simply community.

Genuine, pure, tight-knit, nothing-to-hide, kill-my-best-goat-for-you kind of community.

The church wasn't a place. The church was a group. And wherever the group gathered, the church thrived. As our first example of living out an authentic faith, the early Church clues us in to just how important community is.

In fact, there is a passage in Thessalonians that reveals, almost defines, this early glimpse of community in Paul's own words:

"SO WE CARED FOR YOU. BECAUSE WE LOVED YOU SO MUCH, WE WERE DELIGHTED TO SHARE WITH YOU NOT ONLY THE GOSPEL OF GOD BUT OUR LIVES AS WELL." (1 THESSALONIANS 2:8).

THERE IT IS.

YOUR JOB AS
AN SGL.

YOU CARE.
YOU LOVE.
YOU DELIGHT.

But most importantly, you share—not just the gospel—but your life as well.

God created us for community.
Jesus illustrated community.
The Church practiced community.

THEREFORE, CONNECTING THE FAITH OF YOUR FEW TO A COMMUNITY IS YOUR PRIMARY GOAL. SO, HOW DO YOU CREATE THIS COMMUNITY?

BE PRESENT.

When you lead small you choose to **be present**.
When you choose to be present you **connect** authentic faith.
When you choose to be present that means you . . .

Show up predictably.

Show up mentally.

Show up randomly.

Your very first, basic, fundamental task as an SGL is to

SHOW UP PREDICTABLY.

Show up consistently; for most of you that means weekly.

This is what you signed up for. This is the bare minimum of your job description. But don't let that fool you. It is also the most important thing you can do. Because until you are showing up predictably, consistently, regularly, you cannot check off the rest of the tasks in this book.

You cannot lead a small group without trust.
You cannot build a community without trust.
And the first step to gaining the trust of your few is making sure they know you will show up. Predictably.

Everyone needs someone who is predictable in their life.
* Toddlers need someone who doesn't look like a stranger.
* Elementary schoolers need someone who remembers the name of their goldfish.
* Middle schoolers need someone who is up-to-date on their weekly—sometimes daily—dramas.
* High schoolers need someone who knows their personal struggles and is committed to walking through it all with them.

Everybody needs someone who knows their name, and what's happening in their life

---

So, once you have your mind wrapped around the commitment behind this first task, stay focused. Because your next task involves a wee bit o' brain power.

In order to connect your students' authentic faith to a community, in order to truly be present, you have to

SHOW UP MENTALLY.

So, your bare minimum is to show up predictably—weekly. Now, we take it to the next level.

We aren't just talking about sauntering in, sunglasses on, caramel macchiato in hand. We aren't talking about enduring the message, reading off questions, and closing in prayer. No, we are talking about showing up energetic, fully attentive, and eager to listen.

It's one thing to show up physically. It's an entirely different thing to show up physically and mentally.

When you show up mentally, you leave your email at the door. You accept the fact that your status update and Twitter feed will go unmanned for a couple hours. You resist all urges to mentally plan your next vacation, count the ceiling tiles, or "rest your eyes" for a few minutes.

Instead, you engage with your students. You ask about their lives, as though their high score on Angry Birds or who held hands on the field trip last Friday is the kind of information you live for.

But showing up mentally doesn't stop with discussing the latest video games. When you show up mentally, you also commit to engaging your few in meaningful discussions and to listening, really listening, to what your students have to say. This means knowing the content ahead of time and being mentally prepared to shed some light—some Scriptural insight—into their world.

In order to really show up mentally, you need to be prepared, awake and engaged.

WHEN YOU SHOW UP ON A REGULAR BASIS—PHYSICALLY AND MENTALLY—YOU ARE WELL ON THE WAY TO CONNECTING YOUR STUDENTS TO A COMMUNITY OF BELIEVERS THAT WILL ENCOURAGE AUTHENTIC FAITH.

JOURNAL

Use the space below to record a few things about those in your circle. Go the extra step and bring this journal—or a pen and paper—to your next meeting to record important tidbits about your few.

P	C	S
Record something specific about each one, and make a note about her latest accomplishments.	Record a specific activity that appealed to one of your few. Find out if there is something coming up in his week.	Start a practice of writing down prayer requests. This will help you continue to pray throughout the week and also give you a way to follow up on specific requests.

JOURNAL

NOW THAT YOU
HAVE THE BASICS
DOWN, LET'S MOVE
TO THE THIRD,
MORE ABSTRACT,
AND POTENTIALLY
MORE IMPACTFUL,
WAY TO BE
PRESENT IN THE
LIVES OF
YOUR FEW.

SHOW UP RANDOMLY.

Once you start showing up predictably, your few will begin to expect it. Good. But what if, on occasion, you surprised them? What if you showed up at a time and place they weren't expecting?

A few years ago, there was a high school student interning with me (Tom) and my team. She was sitting in on a meeting to discuss ideas for training SGLs.

As we discussed, brainstormed, contemplated, she suddenly blurted out . . .

"DO YOU WANT TO KNOW THE BEST THING MY SMALL GROUP LEADER EVER DID?"

We all stopped and looked at her. Of course we wanted to know. Why hadn't we thought to ask her—the one person in the room who had grown up in the small group model—about her experience? As we hid our embarrassment, she continued.

"BACK IN FIFTH GRADE I WAS REALLY NERVOUS ABOUT A TEST, AND I MENTIONED IT IN SMALL GROUP. THEN, THE NIGHT BEFORE THE TEST, MY MOM SAID I HAD A PHONE CALL. IT WAS MY SMALL GROUP LEADER. SHE HAD CALLED TO TELL ME SHE WAS THINKING ABOUT AND PRAYING FOR ME AND THAT SHE THOUGHT I WOULD DO GREAT ON THE TEST!"

AS A STAFF, WE WERE AMAZED. HERE WAS A HIGH SCHOOL STUDENT TELLING US ABOUT A SIMPLE PHONE CALL AN SGL MADE MANY YEARS EARLIER. NOT ONLY DID SHE REMEMBER IT . . . SHE DESCRIBED THAT LITTLE PHONE CALL AS THE "BEST THING" HER SGL EVER DID.

NEVER
UNDERESTIMATE
THE POWER OF
SHOWING UP
RANDOMLY.

- A PHONE CALL
- A BIRTHDAY
  CARD
- A BALL GAME
- A TEXT MESSAGE
- A FACEBOOK
  POST
- A POSTCARD
  FROM YOUR TRIP

JOURNAL

Make a list of ways you can show up randomly in the lives of your few. Schedule times to implement your ideas.

P	C	S
On the scheduled time, consider sending a post card with a specific note to the child to show that you are thinking about him.	On the scheduled time, consider sending a note with a picture of something fun that happened in your circle (on your phone or through the mail).	Regularly schedule time to be on Facebook, Twitter or whatever media your students use to connect. Leave them a short message to let them know you are thinking of them. ALSO, plan ahead and show up at their big game, school play or band concert to let them know you really care.

JOURNAL

These small **connections** may seem insignificant. But when
you choose to be present in an unexpected way, outside
of your weekly group time, you reinforce your students'
connection to the community you are creating.

And this sense of community will grow and encourage
authentic faith when you

Show up predictably.

Show up mentally.

Show up randomly.

Your students will begin to trust. They will begin to open up.
They will begin to root themselves in the kind of community—

God designed them to need.
Jesus illustrated with the disciples.
The early church practiced regularly.

You can't be present for everyone. But you can be present for
a few.

That's why the best way to be
present is to **lead small**.

JOURNAL

What are some of the most thoughtful ways others have shown up for you?

Look for opportunities to incorporate some of your ideas to show up predictably, mentally, and randomly.

JOURNAL

JOURNAL

JOURNAL

JOURNAL

2

create
a safe
place

**CLARIFY THEIR FAITH
AS THEY GROW**

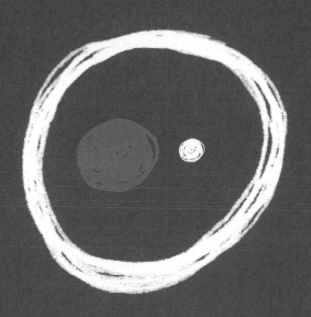

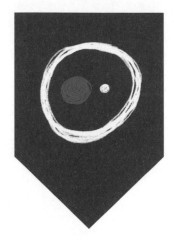

create a safe place

CLARIFY THEIR FAITH AS THEY GROW

So, you have a circle—

Five, eight, maybe ten mini-yous.

And you can't wait to lead them to

Think like you

Talk like you

Act like you in every way.

You are going to spend Saturday afternoons watching all six episodes of *Star Wars*. You are going to share your favorite hiking trails with them. You are all going to buy season passes to the local roller derby bouts. . . .

If you're still nodding your head, maybe you haven't met your few yet.

On the other hand, if you've been with your few for even a couple of

WEEKS
HOURS
MINUTES

you've probably already been disillusioned
(and that's a good thing).

You've already experienced some tension.

It's the inevitable tension created when a group of different people with different personalities and different backgrounds come together in one place. The tension shows up in families. The tension shows up in groups of friends. And you can bet the tension will show up with your few.

Some will love apple juice.
Some will love milk.
Some will love hip hop.
Some will love country.
Some will love the NFL.
Some will love the PGA.

Of course, the tensions won't all be as surface as pop culture and sports. As you go deeper with your few, new, more difficult, tensions will arise.

And one of your most challenging tasks as an SGL is learning to accept and manage the tensions that come up in group.

Your few are very aware of tension. They are watching how you deal with it.
How you deal with it has the potential to give them a sense of security and safety.
As strange as it may seem, **tension is a good thing**.

Tension is actually the platform that gives you an opportunity to demonstrate that this is a safe place.

How you handle **conflict**
How you handle **hard questions**
How you handle **discipline**
How you handle **fears**

You are the leader.
You can't do away with tension.
You can manage it.
You can use it to show kids that this is a safe place.

And the safer your environment is, the more honestly your few will clarify their faith in the context of your circle.

THE MORE YOUR FEW CLARIFY THEIR FAITH, THE CLOSER THEY GET TO DEVELOPING AN AUTHENTIC FAITH THAT WILL STAY WITH THEM BEYOND THEIR GRADUATION DAY. THAT'S WHY ITS SO IMPORTANT TO

CREATE A SAFE PLACE.

When you lead small you choose to **create a safe place**.
When you choose to create a safe place you help your few **clarify** authentic faith.
When you chose to create a safe place, that means you . . .

| Lead the group. | Respect the process. | Guard the heart. |

Small group leaders of little ones know kids will say anything.

"My dad eats his boogers sometimes."
"My mom drank three milkshakes yesterday."
"My friend said God isn't real."

FOR THE MOST PART, YOUNG CHILDREN SIMPLY TRUST YOU BECAUSE YOU ARE OLDER. AND TRUST IS IMPORTANT IF YOU ARE GOING TO HELP YOUR FEW CLARIFY THEIR FAITH. BUT THE TRUTH IS, EVERY YEAR A CHILD GROWS OLDER, THAT TRUST IS HARDER TO EARN. IT'S LIKE THEY START TO HOLD BACK. FILTER. BECOME MORE ... GROWN-UP.

So, how can you earn trust? The first step is to

LEAD YOUR GROUP.

Lead your group to value acceptance.
Lead your group to value confidentiality.
Lead your group to value honesty.

Expect relational tension and set the example you want your few to follow.

If you expect someone to share openly with you, there has to be a foundation of acceptance.

Acceptance can be established in the little things that show how much you care.

Be happy to see them.
Give eye-contact.
Get on their level.
Lean in.

The more often you can be positive and specific, the more you will build an atmosphere of acceptance.

But acceptance is fragile. It's broken by something as subtle as

an eye-roll
a heavy sigh
a knowing smile

The way you handle relational tension sets the tone of acceptance. You can consistently protect your few from the risk of rejection by

celebrating everyone equally
shutting down gossip
privately addressing individual issues as they arise.

And while it may not be realistic for everyone to fully accept each other at all times, the consistent attempt on your part will prove to your few they are in a safe place that values acceptance.

They will feel safe with you.
They will share.
And then their struggles will be tweeted, whispered and immortalized in Jennifer's note to Hannah that gets confiscated and read aloud during science class the next day.

That's where confidentiality comes in.

Confidentiality may be the most difficult to monitor. You typically won't know about a breach until after—

Mark has told the whole football team about Jake's history of bed-wetting.
Tiffany has tweeted about Robyn's disgusting foot fungus.
Ryan has shown the whole class pictures of Justin's blankie.

YOUR JOB IS TO
BALANCE THE
TENSION BETWEEN
ENCOURAGING
CONFIDENTIALITY
AND KNOWING
WHEN TO PROMPT
ONE OF YOUR
FEW TO USE
DISCRETION.

We would all love to have the perfect group filled with
enough respect and maturity to know for sure that what is
said in group stays in group. In fact, that should probably be
a rule you set up in the beginning. Absolute, 100 percent,
swear-on-my-poster-of-Justin-Bieber confidentiality should
always be your goal.

But we have to be realistic. I heard a rumor there was a
breach of confidentiality even in Jesus' circle.
Know your group. When one of your few begins to disclose

something personal *in your circle* that you feel might come back to hurt him later, prompt discretion. Lead the group by asking him to share with you later instead of encouraging him to share juicy details for hungry ears to hear.
(And keep in mind, as the SGL, you can't always promise confidentiality either—but we'll get to that.)

As you lead your group to create a safe place that values acceptance and confidentiality, you have opened the door for another important group characteristic—*honesty.*

Honesty is the only way for your few to

Be themselves

Share doubts

Ask questions

Admit struggles

We could probably write a book just on that list alone and why each of those things is essential for clarifying their faith, but let's just sum up by saying:

IF THEY CAN'T be their Monday-through-Saturday-self when they are with you in group, they will have a hard time applying their faith in everyday situations.
IF THEY CAN'T share their doubts in community, they will dwell on them privately.
IF THEY CAN'T ask you their questions, they are going to ask someone else.
IF THEY DON'T admit their struggles to someone, they will never experience the power of bringing things to light in a way that facilitates freedom and forgiveness.

SO, YOU
ENCOURAGE THE
HONESTY OF YOUR
FEW. YOU REACT
WITH GRACE TO
NEW (SOMETIMES
SHOCKING)
TRUTHS. YOU
PROVE TO THEM
THAT YOUR
INVOLVEMENT
IN THEIR LIVES IS
UNCONDITIONAL.

YOU MODEL
HONESTY IN THE
WAY YOU SHARE
WITH THEM.

Now, about that last statement—*be honest*—as an SGL, have you ever personally struggled with the tension between honesty and inappropriate disclosure?

IN ORDER TO CREATE A SAFE PLACE WHERE YOUR FEW FEEL THEY CAN BE HONEST, IT'S IMPORTANT TO BE HONEST ABOUT YOUR OWN SPIRITUAL, PERSONAL, AND RELATIONAL STRUGGLES— **TO A POINT**.

You need to be aware of their maturity level and stage of life.
The Lion King is terrifying to a two-year-old.
An R-rated movie is taboo for a 4th grader.
Drinking is still illegal for a high school student.

You get the picture. Before you share a personal story,
thought, or anecdote, you may want to ask yourself,

"How will this story benefit them?
What am I trying to accomplish?
Why am I sharing this?"

If the answer to that last question is—

To get them to laugh
To get them to like me
To get their advice
—reconsider.

You can make friends. You can hire a therapist. But your
few will never forget the image of tweety bird tattooed
on your ▮▮▮▮▮

Ankle

JOURNAL

Use the space below to record your mission statement and remind your few of this phrase often.

Since your few might not be ready to write their own mission statement, this looks different for you. Write down specific ways you can make your few feel accepted every week in your circle.

Next time you are together with your few, take the time to come up with a "Group Mission Statement" together. Introduce and discuss the importance of acceptance, confidentiality and honesty. Include these three ideas in your mission statement.

JOURNAL

Now that you are leading the group to value acceptance, confidentiality and honesty, let's add something else to your job as an SGL.

RESPECT THE PROCESS.

There is no checklist for developing an authentic faith in your few. In fact, there is
No finish line.
No plaque.
No medal.
No, "Congratulations! Your few have now achieved authentic faith!"

Instead, authentic faith is a continual process. It's not static. It is the
molding,
crafting,
shaping, and changing of faith through time, life experience and reflection.

And this process isn't the same for everyone.
Each individual is different.

That's why you should expect some intellectual tension.

Some will ask,
 "If God is so 'good,' where do natural disasters fit in?"

Others will wonder,
"If Sunday is a day of rest, where does football fit in?"

Still others will need to understand,
"If God made man the day after He made animals, where do dinosaurs fit in?" .

Maybe the latter question doesn't apply to many but it was definitely a piece of my own process.

WHEN I (TOM) WAS YOUNG, I WAS A VERY INQUISITIVE BOY. I ALWAYS WANTED TO KNOW HOW THINGS WORKED. I WANTED TO KNOW HOW THINGS WERE PUT TOGETHER. I WANTED TO KNOW HOW MY FAITH MESHED WITH THIS WORLD.

So, when it came time to have the discussion about creation and where the world came from, my interest was piqued. My science book and my Bible seemed to be telling me different things.

So, I asked my Sunday school teacher what I thought was a simple question.

"HOW DO THE DINOSAURS FIT INTO THE CREATION STORY?"

My Sunday school teacher got frustrated, which was a surprise to me. And then, in an irritated tone, I got this response:

"YOU JUST HAVE TO HAVE MORE FAITH THAN THAT!"

I was obviously confused. I didn't think I was asking about my faith . . . I was simply eager to understand how God made the dinosaurs and where they all went.

And while I didn't get the answer I was looking for, I learned something else that stuck with me for years.
My lesson was this:

Church is not a safe place to ask questions. It's a place to come when you are already confident about your faith.

Fortunately, I *un*-learned that lesson as I got older and my church experiences were more varied.

Unfortunately, many children and students are still learning this lesson in churches every week.

Every once in a while one of your few will ask a question or make a statement about what they believe that will make you cringe.

"Did God really make the whole world in six days?"

"Will my Buddhist friend go to heaven?"

"How far is 'too far'?"

"Am I supposed to be a Republican?"

Your insides might churn. You will feel the need to "set them straight."

You need to make sure they don't walk out of your group with any uncertainty on this important issue. You need to know they understand Truth.

Right?

BUT WHAT IF
GOD IS DOING
SOMETHING
BIGGER IN THEIR
HEARTS?

WHAT IF GOD'S
PLAN ISN'T TO
MAKE YOU FEEL
ASSURED?

I know that's a risky thing to say. So let me clarify. I believe—

ALL SCRIPTURE IS GOD-BREATHED AND IS USEFUL FOR
TEACHING, REBUKING, CORRECTING AND TRAINING IN
RIGHTEOUSNESS, SO THAT THE SERVANT OF GOD MAY BE
THOROUGHLY EQUIPPED FOR EVERY GOOD WORK.
(2 TIMOTHY 3:16).

Your job is absolutely to help your few connect their faith to
the timeless truth of Scripture. You should open your Bible
together and talk about what it says. But a quick answer isn't
always the best solution.

Questions aren't bad. They are inevitable. In fact, in order to
clarify faith, your few will wrestle with questions. They might
even wrestle with them for longer than the hour you spend
with them once a week. So, **respect their process**.

Your goal isn't to give correct answers to all of their questions,
as though you were some brilliant walking, talking biblical
encyclopedia. Don't miss this:

You don't have to have all the right answers in order to be an SGL.

When you don't have a perfect answer, it's okay to say, "I
don't know." You can tell them what you *do* know. Share your
experiences. Look up Scripture together. Ask your pastor. Go
on a journey with them.

But respect their process and they will learn that just because
they have questions or doubts, doesn't mean they have lost
their faith. It just means, like you, they are in the middle of the
unique process of clarifying authentic faith.

JOURNAL

When one of your few asks a question, your reaction may be as important as any answer you give. Write down three guidelines to help you respond in a way that will allow you to speak the truth in love and honor their process.

JOURNAL

NOW HERE'S THE PART THAT'S TRICKY ABOUT CREATING A SAFE PLACE: WHEN YOU ARE SUCCESSFUL, KIDS WILL TRUST YOU.

And when they trust you they may share something that's above your pay grade.

It may be about home life.
It may be about a boyfriend or girlfriend.
It may be about something the individual is considering.

These are the moments you need to understand that creating a safe place means you . . .

GUARD THE HEART.

Faith is personal. We often process the most difficult times in our lives through the filter of faith. Which is why, as an SGL, you should expect some pretty tough, even shocking things to be revealed during small group time. Things that will create emotional tension.

Your job is to live in the tension between respecting confidentiality and knowing when you need outside help. For this reason, we always put a disclaimer on confidentiality. There is no way for an SGL to promise complete confidentiality. Part of creating a safe place means protecting your few. In some cases, the best way to protect your few is through a breach of confidentiality.

Sometimes we talk about the things above the SGL pay grade as the "three hurts:"

1. BEING HURT
2. HURTING OTHERS
3. HURTING THEMSELVES

When one of your few is being hurt, hurting others, or hurting themselves, it is your responsibility to guard their heart by seeking the help of someone in an authority position. If you are leading in the context of a ministry, you should talk to whoever is in charge right away. They will help you figure out the next steps based on their knowledge of the situation as well as the church's policies. Then you can move forward as part of a qualified team to help the individual.

Some risks are unpreventable. But others—well you can do something about those.

Your few could simultaneously contract a powerful case of lice. You could get an angry call from a mom because your game of "jump or dive" gave her son a bruise the size of Kansas on his chest. You could have to call 911 for a kid reacting to a severe peanut allergy.

That's why every SGL needs to *establish boundaries*. In fact, there's a good chance your church has a list of what some of those boundaries need to be. Here, we'll give you some room to write those down. One of them should probably be: "Don't use a hairbrush for your 'sharing' illustration."

JOURNAL

Who is your "boss" as an SGL? Find that person and ask them what your church's rules are for guarding the heart of your few.

When and who to contact for additional assistance:

Boundaries your church has set to protect you and your few:

JOURNAL

Remember, in order to Create a Safe Place you have to

Lead the group
Respect the process
Guard the heart

Then your few will have the opportunity to open up in the small group environment and **clarify** their faith in a way they never could if you were leading big.

Because the best way to create a safe place is to **lead small**.

JOURNAL

JOURNAL

JOURNAL

JOURNAL

JOURNAL

3

partner with parents

NURTURE AN EVERYDAY FAITH

partner with parents

NURTURE AN EVERYDAY FAITH

For forty years, the Israelites had a consistent, physical, daily reminder of God's presence.

It wasn't a WWJD bracelet.
It wasn't a daily devotional on the back of the toilet.
It wasn't the outline of a fish on their minivan.

It was the
manna from heaven
pillar of clouds by day
pillar of fire by night

No one ever wondered if God still cared.
Of course He did. He provided for them *every day*.

So, when it came time to cross the Jordan into Canaan, Moses knew he would have to prepare the Israelites for the harsh reality of a life without everyday, physical signs from God. Moses called the people together, and here's what he said:

"HEAR, O ISRAEL: THE LORD OUR GOD, THE LORD IS ONE. LOVE THE LORD YOUR GOD WITH ALL YOUR HEART AND WITH ALL YOUR SOUL AND WITH ALL YOUR STRENGTH. THESE COMMANDMENTS THAT I GIVE YOU TODAY ARE TO BE ON YOUR HEARTS. IMPRESS THEM ON YOUR CHILDREN. TALK ABOUT THEM WHEN YOU SIT AT HOME AND WHEN YOU WALK ALONG THE ROAD, WHEN YOU LIE DOWN AND WHEN YOU GET UP. TIE THEM AS SYMBOLS ON YOUR HANDS AND BIND THEM ON YOUR FOREHEADS. WRITE THEM ON THE DOORFRAMES OF YOUR HOUSES AND ON YOUR GATES." (DEUTERONOMY 6:4-9)

On the edge of Canaan, Moses didn't talk about how to set up a new government or give detailed battle plans. Moses gave instructions for preserving everyday faith.

Talk about it

when you sit at home

when you walk along the road

when you lie down

when you get up

It's as if he were saying, "Faith has to be a part of the day-to-day moments. It can't just be something you set aside for one day out of the week. It can't just be something you cling to when times are bad." It's as if Moses knew that the key to an authentic faith was to have an every-day-faith.

And if this was key for the faith of the Israelites, it is still true today for your few.

So, beginning next week, you should take breakfast to your few every day. Spend time in each of their homes. Offer to drive them to lacrosse. Tuck a few in at night.

Okay ... on second thought that's not a great idea.

Maybe we shouldn't skip too quickly over the beginning of Moses' words. "Hear O *Israel*." Moses was talking to the entire nation. The grandmas, the uncles, the tent-makers and even—the parents.

PARTNER WITH PARENTS.

Sometimes, if you're really honest, you might catch yourself
thinking you would be a better parent to one of your few than
the parent they currently have.

Maybe you're right.
And *maybe* you don't know the whole story.

Parenting is hard. Really hard. In fact, I've (Reggie) been a parent
and I've been a church leader. And if I were to take off the church
leader hat for just a minute and talk to you as the dad of four kids
who are now all in their twenties, here's what I would say:

Be careful what you think when you think about the parents of
your few. Remember, this mom, dad, grandparent, foster parent,
step-parent, has been with this child for a long time—maybe
since the beginning. There's a good chance they changed a
diaper or two. They've probably sat in a pediatrician's waiting
room. They've seen more, loved more, cried more, hoped more,
and been hurt more by this child than you ever will.

Regardless of their issues, baggage and brokenness, every parent wants to be a better parent.

I believe this because I've never met a parent who walked out
of the delivery room and said, "I can't wait to ruin this kid's
life." Maybe they're out there. I just haven't met them.

NO MATTER WHAT YOU THINK ABOUT THE PARENTS OF YOUR FEW— CONSERVATIVE, LIBERAL, STRICT, AND LAID-BACK ALIKE—THE REALITY IS THEY HAVE MORE INFLUENCE THAN YOU DO.

They do the waking up, feeding, driving, feeding, and tucking in. So, who is better positioned to have an influence on the faith of your few than their parents?

Assuming you meet with them every week, on average, you will have forty hours a year set aside to spend with your few. The average parent has over 3,000 hours a year to spend with their child.

That's not all. If you're a really *great* SGL, you will be with your few for multiple years. You might even stay in touch as they get older. Maybe you will make an appearance in the back row at their wedding. You could send them a Christmas card or two through the years. But their parent—their parent will be influential long after your group has split. Think about it this way:

At best, you will have temporary influence.
By default, a parent has lifelong influence.

So, you can choose to leave the 3,000 hours on the table. You can ignore the powerful influence that a parent has in the life of a child. Or you can just decide that for the sake of your few, you are going to partner with the parent to nurture authentic, everyday faith.

PARTNER WITH PARENTS.

When you lead small you choose to partner with parents. When you choose to partner with parents you nurture authentic faith.
When you chose to partner with parents, that means you ...

Cue the
parent.

Honor the
parent.

Reinforce
the family.

JOURNAL

You already know what you think about parents—the ways you secretly judge or question their methods. It's best not to write those down. So, let's focus on the positive. What are two *benefits* of partnering with parents?

Maybe you should tie those to your hands, your foreheads, your doorposts and gates.

JOURNAL

If you want to partner with parents and tap into those 3,000 hours, you need to first

CUE THE PARENT.

I'm not talking about the queue of parents waiting outside because prayer requests took an extra 15 minutes. This is not about organizing your drop-off and pick-ups to be more efficient.

No, when you "cue" the parent, you give them just the right information at just the right time so they can make a move to do more than they would otherwise do.

So, what's your first cue? It's a tough one.
You might want to write this one down.

Let them know who you are.

Okay, not just your name, but who you are as an SGL. Chances are, they haven't read a book about being an SGL. They might even think of you as their child's Sunday school teacher—yikes! Help them out.

Let them know **that you are planning to show up in their kid's life predictably, and randomly (that will help avoid awkward questions later when they see a stranger with a tweety bird tattoo show up at Johnny's baseball game to cheer him on.)**

Let them know **your goal is to help their child grow in authentic faith.**

Let them know **that you want to help them win as a parent.**

Another cue you should give a parent is a heads up on what you're talking about in your circle. Most parents are looking for more opportunities and ways to connect with their child.

But most conversations consist of:

"How was school?"
"Fine."

"What did you learn in church?"
"'bout God."

"How's the foul shot coming?"
"Good."

What if the parents of your few never had to ask, "What did you learn in church?" What if they already knew enough to begin their conversations on a deeper level?

"Did you learn something about Jonah today?"
"I heard you learned about being a good friend today. What was that about?"

Simply cueing a parent to know a little about the concepts you are discussing in your circle can significantly impact the way a parent can continue having similar conversations at home.

JOURNAL

The key to being able to cue the parent is establishing open communication from the beginning. If you haven't already, introduce yourself to the parents of your few. Explain your role in their child's life, and let them know you want to be a resource to them.

Say something positive and specific about their child to let them know that you genuinely care. Ask them what they think you should know about their child.

In your next small group meeting, have students fill out the following information about their parents.

JOURNAL

Name

Email

Phone number

Address

Occupation

Vehicle

You never know when this information will come in handy.
The address, and vehicle, could be invaluable if you are ever
looking for someone who can help with group transportation.

Cueing the parent is pretty easy—let them know who you are, and tell them what you're talking about. We're easing you in. This next one can be pretty tough because there will be times when it's up to you to protect the relationship between parent and child. In other words, you are going to have to HONOR THE PARENT.

Some children struggle with authority.
No, scratch that.
All children struggle with authority.

"You can't make me eat my broccoli! I'm a big girl!"
"Why do I still have to go to bed at *eight*? In case you haven't noticed, I'm almost nine!"
"*Everyone* in the seventh grade has an iPhone!"

Although it seems like these are prime opportunities to win some cool points—

"Try feeding your veggies to the dog when no one's looking."
"They may make you sit in your bed but they can never make you go to sleep."
"I have an old iPhone you can have."

As their SGL, don't use the week-to-week battles your few have with their parents to gain relational points. Every week can be a rollercoaster of emotions, but remember your job is to help them honor their parents. After all, the Bible commands it. And as the SGL, you are called to help your few apply biblical truth. So, how can they possibly learn to honor mom and dad if you, their SGL, won't model it? (Wait, that's next chapter.)

I (Reggie) have a friend who used to be an elementary school teacher. Every year during open house she would make a deal with the parents of her new students. Here's what she'd say:

"THERE WILL BE DAYS YOUR KIDS COME HOME WITH SOME PRETTY WILD STORIES ABOUT WHAT WENT ON IN SCHOOL. HERE'S WHAT I'D LIKE: BEFORE YOU EMAIL ME, CONSIDER THE POSSIBILITY THAT YOU MAY NOT HAVE HEARD THE WHOLE STORY. AND I'LL TELL YOU WHAT, I'LL DO THE SAME FOR YOU WHEN THEY SHARE STORIES FROM HOME."

I think that's a pretty genius trade. It assumes that every story has more than one perspective. It assumes that the precious children we love may not always give the most accurate portrayal of a situation. Maybe you need to have a similar agreement with the parents of your few.

Some conflicts will be bigger than just a struggle over soggy broccoli. And some of the stories can be hard to swallow. We don't want to make light of the fact that some of your few may struggle with some pretty serious issues at home.

But remember this:

if you're not on the parent's side, you're not on the kid's side.

I'm sure you're thinking, *Now wait a minute! That doesn't even make sense. You don't understand the situation!*

I'm pretty sure we covered some of those things in the last chapter, but for everything else, here's what I mean: If a parent is the greatest influence in a child's life, and if that parent will have lifelong influence, then it makes sense to always build a bridge.

Ten, fifteen, twenty years down the road, the way a child learns to handle conflict with his or her parent will affect that child's
Dating
Marriage
Parenting
Sense of self
Authentic faith

So, build a bridge. One of my favorite examples of this happened a few years ago. One of our high school students was in a knock-down-drag-out fight with her parents over her grades. There was yelling. Things were said that probably didn't need to be said. In a final fury the parents sent this girl to her room and told her not to come out.

While in her room she did something that I love.
She called her SGL.

Through tears she angrily expressed how unfair and horrible her parents were. The punishments they were suggesting were *way* out of line. The things they said were *way* too harsh. After all, she was a good kid. Why didn't they see that?

Her SGL listened while she talked. And then delicately, sympathetically, the SGL started to ask some questions. The conversation went something like this:

"YOU ARE A GOOD KID. I'VE TALKED TO YOUR MOM, AND SHE KNOWS THAT. SHE BELIEVES IN YOU. SO, WHY DO YOU THINK SHE'S SO UPSET RIGHT NOW?"

"HAVE YOU REALLY BEEN WORKING AS HARD AS YOU SHOULD ON YOUR SCHOOL WORK? ARE THERE OTHER THINGS THAT HAVE BEEN DISTRACTING YOU?"

As the conversation progressed, the girl's anger subsided. She started to think more clearly about the position her parents were in. She acknowledged that she was part of the problem. Then she and her SGL put together an action plan. At the suggestion of the SGL, the girl outlined everything that she was going to do to help get her grades back under control. She made suggestions for her own punishment based on what she knew were her primary distractions. Then she walked back downstairs—plan in hand, new attitude.

THE SGL SAW AN
OPPORTUNITY TO
BUILD A BRIDGE
AND CHOSE TO
HONOR THE
PARENTS.

Now, there's just one more way for an SGL to partner with parents. The final step in partnering with parents is finding ways to

REINFORCE THE FAMILY.

Although parents potentially have 3,000 hours a year of possible time with their child, it's not always the same quality as the hours you have with your few.

Those 3,000 hours are filled with

Making dinner
Cramming for spelling tests
Driving to and from practice
Watching *Cars* for the fifth time in one week so mom can do the laundry

But your forty hours are potentially filled with

Meaningful conversations
Teachable moments
Bonding experiences

Since you have such little time, you tend to make the most of it. But don't get greedy. There are some times, experiences, and conversations that parents want to be a part of.

Christmas Eve isn't a good time for a group slumber party. You probably shouldn't be the first person to have "the talk." You might even reconsider before inviting your few over for an epic weekend of *Star Wars*.

I (Tom) will never forget the moment my son first watched *Star Wars*.

I had been waiting for the day Mac was old enough to embark on this epic journey with me. *Star Wars* was the first movie I remember seeing. And for some reason, more than 30 years later, my heart still beats fast when I hear the "Imperial March." I was having trouble trying to decide if I should show it to him in the order the story happens—Episode 1-6 or if should I show it in the order I saw it? But I never got to decide.

The reason I'll never forget the moment my son first watched Star Wars is because I wasn't there.

He came home from a sleepover having watched *Return of the Jedi* with his friend. (Talk about out of order!)

As disappointed as I was, I couldn't help thinking, "what if it had been a more meaningful experience?"

Sometimes, without meaning to, it's easy for an SGL to get greedy in the experiences they want to share with their few. When you are intentionally reinforcing the family, you will include parents in big decisions like a moment of salvation or a baptism.

EVEN IF THE PARENT ISN'T A BELIEVER, THEY ARE STILL THE PARENT, AND INCLUDING THEM IN THESE EXPERIENCES HAS THE POTENTIAL TO MAKE A MORE MEANINGFUL IMPACT IN THE LIVES OF YOUR FEW.

> **JOURNAL**

Sometimes your job is to cue the parents to know how to connect. Other times, you can cue one of your few to go connect with their family. Brainstorm some topics that might come up in your circle that would be a good opportunity to cue your few to connect with their parents.

JOURNAL

There are some days on the calendar that are just special days for family. List those days here as a reminder NOT to schedule time with your few on these occasions.

> # REMEMBER, YOUR ROLE IN THEIR LIFE IS TEMPORARY; THE PARENT'S INFLUENCE IS LIFELONG.

There are many ways to reinforce the family so get creative. And as long as you keep the family relationship in the forefront of your mind, you will successfully partner with the parents through

Cueing the parent

Honoring the parent

Reinforcing the family

This is a big job—a job that a senior pastor cannot do. Why? Because it's a job for someone devoted to nurturing the faith of a few. Someone like you who chose to lead small.

The best way to partner with parents is to **lead small**.

JOURNAL

JOURNAL

JOURNAL

JOURNAL

JOURNAL

4

make it personal

INSPIRE THEIR FAITH BY YOUR EXAMPLE

make it personal

INSPIRE THEIR FAITH BY YOUR EXAMPLE

We all naturally look to others for examples of—
What to wear
What to eat
Where to vacation
What to believe

Okay, maybe some of you don't like that. I can feel you pushing back already.

"I am my own person, thank you very much. I do what I want, wear what I want and think how I want."

Fine. Maybe you are independent. Maybe you are a free thinker. But I bet your mouth still waters a little when you see a commercial with a plate of sizzling fajitas.

And I wouldn't doubt if your few influence you in ways you may or may not realize—
Maybe you bought that new video game for your nephew that someone was talking about in group.
Maybe you stopped wearing white tube socks after your few deemed them "gross."
Maybe you reverted back to saying, "I need to go potty."

(If that last one is true, you should really get some new friends—preferably over the age of five.)

There's no denying the power of example. And if it can inspire you—*trendsetting, groundbreaking, trailblazing you*—it will be sure to inspire the minds of your few.

THAT'S WHY, AS AN SGL, YOUR JOB GOES BEYOND YOUR SCHEDULED MEETINGS. IT GOES BEYOND BOWLING OUTINGS AND STARBUCKS CONVERSATIONS. IT GOES BEYOND EMAILING PARENTS.

IT'S ABOUT THE EXAMPLE YOU ARE SHOWING THEM THROUGH YOUR OWN LIFE.

The example you are setting for your few through the way you live your personal life is just as important as those hand-drawn postcards you send out on their birthdays.

That's why we are going to take some time to Make it Personal.

This is all about you.
Your free time.
Your life away from your few.

Because the most important thing you need to lead is not your few—it's actually you.

As it turns out, being an SGL is a little more complex than you first thought.

Already you have to pay attention in the circle, randomly connect outside the circle, and partner with their parents. What more could be expected? A 3,000-word reflective essay on the developmental patterns of your few to be turned into your supervisor quarterly?

No. Just the small task of making sure your personal life is in order—making sure you are living an example you want your few to follow.

Your few have a front-row seat to your life. The question is, what are they watching? Is it just a show? Or is it a real-life adventure pursuing God? What if watching your personal growth could really be their front-row seat to what God wants to do in their lives?

IF YOU WANT YOUR FEW TO HAVE HEALTHY RELATIONSHIPS, THEY NEED TO SEE IT IN YOU.
IF YOU WANT YOUR FEW TO SET BOUNDARIES, THEY NEED TO SEE IT IN YOU.
IF YOU WANT YOUR FEW TO BE CONFIDENT IN WHO GOD MADE THEM TO BE, THEY NEED TO SEE IT IN YOU.

MAKE IT PERSONAL.

When you lead small you choose to **make it personal**.
When you choose to make it personal you **inspire** authentic faith.
When you choose to make it personal that means you . . .

| Live in Community. | Set Priorities. | Be Real. |

In the book, *Parenting Beyond Your Capacity*, we outline five big ideas for parents. And making it personal is the one skill that bridges across both parenting and leading small.

Making it personal is essential for anyone who wants to have an impact on the faith of the next generation because, guess what?

They have a very acute "fake detector."

> # IF YOU TRY TO BE SOMEONE IN YOUR CIRCLE THAT ISN'T CONSISTENT WITH WHO YOU REALLY ARE WHEN YOU AREN'T IN YOUR CIRCLE, YOU WILL EVENTUALLY BE FOUND OUT BY THE ONES YOU LEAD.

When Timothy was a young leader of the church in Ephesus, his SGL, mentor, Paul, reminds him—

DON'T LET ANYONE LOOK DOWN ON YOU BECAUSE YOU ARE YOUNG, BUT SET AN EXAMPLE FOR THE BELIEVERS IN SPEECH, IN LIFE, IN LOVE, IN FAITH AND IN PURITY, (1 TIMOTHY 4:13).

As an SGL—whether you are young or just young at heart—you are called to set an example in the way you live out your life.

And one of the most important things you can do for yourself is to

LIVE IN COMMUNITY.

I know what you're thinking. And no, your small group of three-year-olds does not count as your "community."

You can't sort out your struggles over a pile of goldfish and a Dixie cup of apple juice.

You are the "grown-up" for your few. You can share appropriate pieces of your life at appropriate times but your few cannot be expected to fuel you in the way your own adult group can.

Whether hosted by your church, formed organically, or brought together through another local ministry, your own community provides the healthy—and necessary—outlet for you to process faith in a way you can't with your few.

The small group you have formed with your few is for them.

The community you live in with your peers is for you.

AND THE MORE
YOU ARE ABLE TO
LEAN ON YOUR
OWN COMMUNITY,
THE LESS YOU WILL
BE TEMPTED TO
BLUR THOSE LINES
WHEN YOU ARE
WITH YOUR FEW.

JOURNAL

Use this space to make a list of a few people who are or could be your community. Are they in a similar stage of life? Are they a little further down the road?
Would they understand your struggles?
Do you feel comfortable sharing with them?
Would you respect their input?

JOURNAL

If you are having trouble coming up with a list, take some time to research the opportunities your church offers to connect its members to a community.

The second step to making it personal—to inspiring the faith of your few through example—requires you to

SET PRIORITIES.

Have you ever lost sight of what really matters in life? All of a sudden you realize:

You haven't slept more than four hours in the past week. It's been three days since you brushed your teeth. You've eaten nothing but Big Macs for a month.

Okay, maybe that's a little extreme. But the point is, we all have a tendency to get distracted and forget what's really important.

One of the best things you can do for your few—and for yourself—is to make your priorities clear. They need to see what you value. And when they see the way you prioritize your life, it might even inspire your few to think about their own priorities.

The first priorities you set should be

Spiritual priorities.

This should come as a no-brainer to you. You are leading your few to grow spiritually. You should also be invested in your own continual spiritual growth.

No matter the age of your few, this is true:

The only way you will effectively be able to discuss authentic faith with your few is if you are experiencing authentic faith in your own life.

IF YOU ARE SIMPLY
TRYING TO INSTILL
FAITH AND MORALS
FOR THE SAKE OF
YOUR FEW, BUT IT'S
NOT A PERSONAL
PRIORITY, THEY'LL
EVENTUALLY
CATCH ON.

We have five things we say are really important skills to help kids grow their faith. And, when you think about it, many kids will practice these skills—even learn these skills for the first time—with their SGL. But these skills aren't just for your few. These skills span across all ages—they are true in your faith as well as the faith of your few.

We've got a really catchy name for them—we call them

the 5 Faith Skills:

Navigate the Bible
(survey and locate Scripture)

Personalize Scripture
(memorize and apply)

Dialogue with God
(pray in private and public)

Articulate Faith
(share and defend)

Worship with Your Life
(praise and give)

These are not only the things you should encourage your few to do; these are the things you should be doing in your own life.

How can you encourage your few to spend time reading their Bible each day, if yours is currently used as a coaster on your coffee table?

How can you promote the memorization of Scripture, if you can't remember the beginning of John 3:16?

How can you emphasize the power of prayer, if the only prayer in your life is the one your son recites before dinner?

How can you point out the benefits of discussing their faith with others, if your motto is "never talk about religion, politics or money."

How can you push your few to live out their faith, if you never serve, praise or give?

THE ANSWER IS, YOU CAN'T. IN ORDER TO INSPIRE AUTHENTIC FAITH IN YOUR FEW, YOU MUST FIRST PRACTICE AND PRIORITIZE AUTHENTIC FAITH IN YOUR OWN LIFE.

But your spiritual life is not the only thing you need to put first. You should also set

Relational priorities.

There are people in your life that should always come before your few. Yes, you heard that right: your few should be priorities but not the priority. True, you should probably put them before your pharmacist, mailman or Starbucks barista.

But sometimes

having a date night with your spouse
choosing to take your kids to the park
picking up a friend with a flat tire
skipping group to celebrate your mom's 60th birthday
or leaving a small group retreat because your sister is in labor

says more than always putting your few first. You need to focus on the important relationships in your life because no one can be the

spouse
parent
friend
child
sibling

that you are. And when you put significance on those people in your life, you are modeling healthy relationships for your few. You are a physical, living, breathing example of someone who

dates their spouse
spends quality time with their children
is there for their friends
respects and honors their parents
and values their siblings.

AND WHEN
YOU SET THESE
PRIORITIES—BOTH
SPIRITUAL AND
RELATIONAL—YOU
EMPHASIZE AND
INSPIRE A HEALTHY
LIFESTYLE FOR
YOUR FEW.

JOURNAL

It's impossible to live by your spiritual and relational priorities if you never decide what they are.

Review the 5 Faith Skills. What is one thing you are currently doing to invest in your own spiritual growth?

JOURNAL

Some relationships are more important than others. Have you ever really thought about that? List the relationships in your life that you should put first—even before your few.

The last—and possibly most important—way to inspire the authentic faith of your few is to

BE REAL.

Okay, so "most important" may sound like an overstatement compared to honoring your parents and reading your Bible. But think about it this way: None of those things will really inspire authentic faith if you are not "real" with your few.

In other words, they will never truly see how you live in community and how you prioritize your life, if you are too busy pretending to

be scared of the boogie man
be a world-class ollie expert
or love vampire fiction.

Your few don't need another peer. Your few need a leader. A role model. And that means it's okay if you don't do what they do, think what they think or like what they like all the time.

Be real. Find ways to relate to your few without compromising who you really are. Because it's more important for them to see a real, live person that is still growing, learning, and trying to live out authentic faith than it is for them to have another friend.

Leading small helps you keep your world manageable. It allows you to focus on staying real in your own faith. When you lead small you have time and margin to

Live in Community

Set Priorities

Be Real

You have the ability to show the authenticity of your own faith to a few to **inspire** their faith.

That's why the best way to make it personal is to **lead small**.

JOURNAL

JOURNAL

JOURNAL

JOURNAL

5

move them out

ENGAGE THEIR FAITH IN A
BIGGER STORY

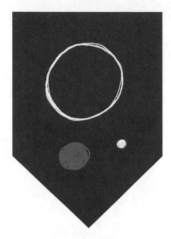

move them out

ENGAGE THEIR FAITH IN
A BIGGER STORY

We are not meant to be stagnant. Life moves at a dizzying pace.

We go from kindergarten to graduating high school in a little over a decade.
We finish college and begin our careers in less than half that time.
Before long, we are ushered into credit scores, job promotions, senior discounts, and a nice one-story beach house in Florida.

Your few are no exception. In the next ten years,
They will not be wearing hair bows.
They will no longer believe in the Tooth Fairy.
They will trade their Nintendo for car keys.
They will move out into college dorms or apartments and eventually their own homes.

As if those realizations aren't hard enough to wrap your mind around, here's one that is possibly even harder for you to accept:

You will no longer be their SGL.

That's right, they will have different SGLs, role models, interests and hobbies. So, while you are leading your few through this small chapter of their lives, it's important to think about their lives outside of your circle. It's important to think about the adults they are becoming.

WHEN YOU FOCUS ON THE BIGGER STORY OF THEIR LIVES, YOU UNDERSTAND THAT WHAT HAPPENS INSIDE YOUR CIRCLE IS MEASURED BY WHAT HAPPENS OUTSIDE YOUR CIRCLE. THE INCREDIBLE POTENTIAL OF LEADING SMALL REALLY IS IN YOUR ABILITY TO

MOVE THEM OUT.

When you lead small you choose to **move them out**.
When you choose to move them out you **engage** authentic faith.
When you chose to move them out, that means you . . .

Move them
to someone
else.

Move them
to be the
Church.

Move them
to what's
next.

There's a lot going on inside your circle. But there's also a lot going on in the lives of your few outside your circle.

They have other friends.

They have other activities.

And (brace yourself) they have other

role models.

As an SGL, it's easy to get protective of your few. And sometimes that protective feeling can morph into jealousy. You want to be the one they call when they have

Problems with friends

Questions about God

Trouble at home

But the truth is, your few might also be connected to a really cool uncle, a wise neighbor, a favorite teacher, or even (drum roll . . .) another SGL.

That's okay!

Not only is that okay, that's your first goal in moving them out. You have to look for ways to

MOVE THEM TO SOMEONE ELSE.

We have already explained (very delicately) that you will not be their SGL forever. So, of course your few will need another leader in their life at some point. But that's not all that we are saying.

The truth is, today, as we speak, while you are still their SGL, your few need other positive adult influences in their lives.

In fact, what we've found is that a growing number of experts are saying, the more Christian adult influences a child has, the more likely it will be for that child to stay connected to church after graduation.

This doesn't mean that a kid needs ten SGLs.
A child doesn't need ten small group leaders any more than they need ten moms.

THE POINT IS
THIS—
YOUR FEW ARE
GOING TO
CONNECT WITH
OTHER LEADERS
WHO WILL
TEACH THEM
SOMETHING
ABOUT GOD,
HELP THEM
DISCOVER
SOMETHING
ABOUT LIFE,
EXPERIENCE
SOMETHING
SIGNIFICANT
TOGETHER.

YOU ARE IN A UNIQUE ROLE TO HELP CELEBRATE AND ENCOURAGE THOSE RELATIONSHIPS.

SO, MOVE THEM TO SOMEONE OUTSIDE OF YOUR CIRCLE. DO YOUR PART TO ENCOURAGE OTHER ADULT INFLUENCES IN THEIR LIVES.

 **JOURNAL**

Use this space to list some important adult influences you had as you were growing up. Who else has the potential to influence the life of a child?

Think about your few. Make a list of the people you know who are a positive influence in their lives. Make an effort to speak positively about these individuals and encourage these relationships.

JOURNAL

NOT ONLY SHOULD YOU MOVE YOUR FEW TO **SOMEONE** OUTSIDE YOUR CIRCLE, YOU SHOULD ALSO MOVE YOUR FEW TO DO **SOMETHING** OUTSIDE YOUR CIRCLE.

Your circle is a great place to experience the church. For some of you, your circle will be the first impression your few ever have of church. But if your few grow up in church and they only ever sit in circles, they will have missed out on something pretty significant.

That's why your next task is to

MOVE THEM TO BE THE CHURCH.

"Being" the Church has nothing to do with improv, a game of charades or a Halloween costume involving a large cardboard box.

This is about connecting and *engaging* your few with a bigger story—encouraging them to not just attend church but to be part of participating in the mission of the church.

In this sense, the Church is more than just a building or a location. The Church is a growing, changing, moving, living being that your few get to be a part of.

Never underestimate the importance of letting them—
Pass out goldfish at snack time
Participate in telling the Bible story
Lead worship for younger kids

If your few are older, their participation should be more involved. They can—
Adopt a local charity as a small group
Be an SGL for younger kids
Help with service planning or production

The options are endless.

This may sound like a daunting task. You may think it will be hard to convince your few to serve in their free time when they could be—
Riding their bikes
Playing video games
Or texting their friends

But you would be surprised how quickly your few jump
on board.

Kids want to feel significant. Really, we all want to feel significant, but kids *especially* want to feel significant. They want to prove they can do something more than unload the silverware caddy in the dishwasher. (Although, that may still be a high achievement for some of your few.)

They are still searching for the place they fit in but the reality is—

A CHILD WILL
NEVER FEEL
SIGNIFICANT
UNTIL YOU
GIVE THEM
SOMETHING
SIGNIFICANT
TO DO.

I (Reggie) know an SGL of high school girls that understood this principle and used the time she was given to show her girls what it meant to be the Church.

Each year, the student ministry held a retreat at the church. The SGLs would stay at homes with their few and travel to the church for sessions in the morning and evening. Each Saturday, the schedule allowed room for a five-hour free time, and the church would provide $15 per student so the SGLs could take their few paintballing, shopping, bowling, etc., in order to have down-time together to solidify the relationships.

While I still think there is value in all of those things, this particular leader decided to use the time (and money) the church provided to do something a little different. Instead of sitting in pedicure chairs or buying matching bracelets, she made a tradition of using those five hours to volunteer—as a group. They cleaned homeless shelters, prepared meals, and planted inner-city gardens. Not only that, they combined their $15 each and donated it to the charity they helped serve.

When it came time for dinner back at the church, her girls showed up with dirt under their nails, leaves in their hair, and smelling of sweat. But you know what?

They felt significant.

We cannot underestimate that feeling of being important in someone else's life. As an SGL, it's your job to introduce them to that feeling—to encourage them to move outside the circle and get involved. In fact, this may be one of the best strategies when facing that BIG challenge we talked about at the beginning of the book. **Because what we have found is that if they aren't being the Church when they are with us, they won't know how to be a part of the Church when they leave us.**

JOURNAL

Write down some ways you could let your few become "helpers" in your circle. Try to give your few as many opportunities to serve within your circle as possible.

Find out what opportunities your church has to let children get involved serving others. Tell the parents of your few about these opportunities and encourage their participation.

In what areas of your church could your few volunteer regularly? Next time you are with your few, talk about these opportunities.

JOURNAL

Research a few local charities. List them here.

Next time you are with your few, discuss some ways and times to get involved in volunteering and "being the Church" together.

So, now you're ready to move them to someone else and move them to do something significant. But what about that unsettling thing we mentioned earlier? What about the day when you are no longer their SGL?

Whether you are the leader of a toddler group or a group of high school seniors teetering on the edge of adulthood, you should always be looking forward. You should always be aware of what is next for your few. And you should be looking for ways to ease these transitions—ways to

MOVE THEM TO WHAT'S NEXT.

**Are your few about to
Start school?
Graduate Kindergarten?
Move into middle school?
Get their driver's license?
Go to college?**

No matter what is next in their lives, it is your responsibility to do everything you can to set them up for that transition and make sure it goes as smoothly as possible.

If they are moving into a new circle for first grade . . .
Maybe you can hand their new SGL something specific and positive about each individual in your group.

If they are facing the big halls of middle school . . .
Maybe you can bring in a team of resident eighth grade experts to share a little bit about what it's like in a world with lockers and vending machines.

If they are filling out college applications . . .
Maybe you can plan to clear your calendar for an extra year, to walk them through one of the most significant transitions of their life.

Our church asks high school SGLs to commit to stay with their circle for four years. When we made a decision to ask for that level of commitment, I was a little nervous. Four years is a long time. Looking back, I can't imagine leading students any other way.

A few years ago, an SGL I (Reggie) know did something I hadn't seen before. She went through four years of high school with her circle of girls. She saw the ups and downs. She helped them through confusing times and celebrated their accomplishments. Then, graduation day came. The church gave her a small token of appreciation for her service and her job was over—but something wasn't right. If she simply started back over with a freshman group, she would be disconnecting right when the stakes were the highest. She would be sacrificing her relational influence when the felt need was the greatest.

So, she went to the youth minister and asked if she could spend an extra year with her girls—a fifth year making sure their transition to college was smooth.

She spent that year staying connected through social media, visiting college campuses, connecting her few to a local church, and planning get-togethers over the holidays.

Not every SGL is wired for a five-year commitment. But don't miss the point.

No matter the age or stage of your few, they will eventually face a life transition. How you prepare them for and walk them through that time can ease the growing pains and anxiety to make them feel more comfortable about what's next.

JOURNAL

What stage of life are your few in? Use this space to list a few big milestones coming up for them.

JOURNAL

Brainstorm any fears or anxieties they could have around
these milestones and ways you could help cushion
the transition.

When you move them out, you **engage** them in a bigger story. You are responsible for holding five, ten, maybe fifteen hands as they meet new role models, discover their significance, and transition through life.

Your job is to

Move them to someone else

Move them to be the church

Move them to what is next

It's a big job.

But it's not a job for someone who thinks big. It's a job for someone who can fully invest in these lives by leading small.

The best way to move them out is to **lead small**.

JOURNAL

JOURNAL

JOURNAL

JOURNAL

JOURNAL

conclusion

CONCLUSION

So when you lead small you

Connect authentic faith

Clarify authentic faith

Engage authentic faith

Nurture authentic faith

Inspire authentic faith

That's a really big job. It's not the kind of job you sign up for if you're just looking to kill an extra hour a week doing something mindless—there are a lot of other great options for that.

This is a journey that you sign up for because
You want to do something significant.
You are ready to make a difference.
You care about the authentic faith of the next generation.

And as an SGL, you will make a difference.

How can we be so confident?

Your job as an SGL can all be boiled down to one very simple thought. One phrase. One idea.

In fact, mark this page.

So, when you feel overwhelmed, when you feel stuck, when you feel paralyzed, open the book to this page and know that all you have to remember is

Your few are not problems to be solved. They are people to be loved.

When you love them, you will *connect* by showing up predictably, mentally and randomly.
When you love them, you will naturally create a safe place for them to *clarify their faith*.
When you love them, you will partner with others who love them in order to *nurture* an everyday faith.
When you love them, you will want to *inspire* them through your example.
When you love them, you will *engage* their faith with things outside of your circle.

The best way to love your few is to **lead small**.

Continue this conversation at **www.LeadSmall.org**.

AUTHOR BIOS

REGGIE JOINER

Reggie Joiner is founder of Orange, a team of innovative writers, creators, and doers who are devoted to influencing those who influence the next generations. He is one of the founding pastors of North Point Community Church in Alpharetta, Ga. In his 11 years as the executive director of Family Ministry, Reggie led a staff to create relevant environments and resources for preschoolers, children, students, and married adults. His other books include *Seven Practices of Effective Ministries, Think Orange, Parenting Beyond Your Capacity, The Orange Leader Handbook,* and *The Orange Wardrobe: How to Incorporate Orange-wear 24/7/365.* (Okay, that last one hasn't made it off the editor's desk yet.) Reggie and his wife, Debbie are currently paying for all four of their children to finish college. He's seriously considering working the late shift at Starbucks.

TOM SHEFCHUNAS

Tom is the North Point Ministries Multi-Campus Director of Transit (Middle School). Tom's passion involves working with the campus directors and their teams, as well as recruiting and developing the hundreds of volunteer small group leaders it takes to pull off Transit at the five campuses. He is also the co-founder of www.UthMin.net, an online community of strategic student leaders. Tom and his wife Julie live in Cumming, Georgia, with their three children, Mac, Joey and Cooper.